KS2
Grammar, Punctuation and Spelling

SATs
Question Book

KS2
Grammar,
Punctuation
and Spelling
SATs
Question Book

Shelley Welsh

Contents

Grammar

Punctuation

Spelling and Vocabulary

- The questions in this book are divided into sections: grammar, punctuation, and spelling and vocabulary.

- There are different types of question for you to answer in different ways. The space for your answer shows you what type of answer is needed.

- Some questions are multiple choice and may require a tick in the box next to the answer; some require a word or phrase to be underlined or circled, while others have a line or box for the answer. Some questions ask for missing punctuation to be inserted.

- Always read the instructions carefully so that you know how to answer each question.

- All questions are worth 1 mark.

- There are three progress tests throughout the book to allow you to practise the skills again. Record your results in the progress charts to identify what you are doing well in and what you can improve.

Acknowledgements

Every effort has been made to trace copyright holders and obtain their permission for the use of copyright material. The author and publisher will gladly receive information enabling them to rectify any error or omission in subsequent editions. All facts are correct at time of going to press.

Published by Collins
An imprint of HarperCollins*Publishers*
1 London Bridge Street
London SE1 9GF

© HarperCollins*Publishers* Limited 2016

ISBN 9780008201609

First published 2016

10

All rights reserved. No part of this publication may be reproduced, stored in a retrieval system, or transmitted, in any form or by any means, electronic, mechanical, photocopying, recording or otherwise, without the prior permission of Collins.

British Library Cataloguing in Publication Data. A CIP record of this book is available from the British Library.

Commissioning Editor: Michelle I'Anson
Author: Shelley Welsh
Project Management and Editorial: Fiona Kyle and Katie Galloway
Cover Design: Sarah Duxbury and Amparo Barrera
Inside Concept Design: Paul Oates and Ian Wrigley

Text Design and Layout: Contentra Technologies
Production: Lyndsey Rogers
Printed and bound in China by RR Donnelley APS

MIX
Paper from responsible source
FSC www.fsc.org FSC™ C007454

This book is produced from independently certified FSC™ paper to ensure responsible forest management.

For more information visit:
www.harpercollins.co.uk/green

Word Classes – Nouns, Adjectives, Adverbs and Verbs

1 Complete the sentence below with an **adjective** formed from the verb **apologise**.

My sister was very <u>Sorry</u>_____ after
she spilled water on my painting.

1 mark

2 Write a sentence below using the word **light** as a **noun**.

Remember to punctuate your answer correctly.

<u>Light was streaming in through the open door.</u>

_____

Write a sentence below using the word **light** as a **verb**.

Remember to punctuate your answer correctly.

_____

_____

1 mark

3 Write the correct label in each box below to show the **word class**.

verb	noun	adjective	adverb
A	B	C	D

Our new kitten slept peacefully through the night.

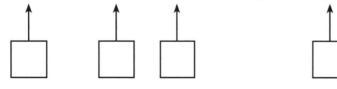

1 mark

Word Classes – Nouns, Adjectives, Adverbs and Verbs

Tick one box in each row below to show whether the underlined word is an **adjective** or an **adverb**.

Sentence	Adjective	Adverb
The car drove very <u>fast</u> round the corner.		
We approached the tunnel's <u>wide</u> opening.		
Maddie is wearing the <u>wrong</u> shoes!		
We arrived <u>early</u> for the show.		

1 mark

Insert a suitable **adverb** into the sentence below.

Kai watered the plants _____ .

1 mark

6 Circle the **two adverbs** in the sentence below.

Sam was possibly going to arrive late.

1 mark

Total marks .... /6   How am I doing? ☺ 😐 ☹

Pronouns and Possessive Pronouns

1 Circle the **pronoun** in the sentence below.

(I) walked to school because the bus didn't arrive.

1 mark

2 Complete the sentence below with a **possessive pronoun**.

Please give me those books back – they are _theirs_____!

1 mark

3 Complete the sentences below using the **pronouns I** or **me**.

My brother told _me_____ to hurry up.

Our teacher explained the method to Mia and _I_____.

It was raining when Dan and _I_____ finally went into the playground.

Mum and _me_____ finished eating then went for a walk.

1 mark

4 Write a **pronoun** that could be used to replace the underlined word in the passage below. Do not change the meaning of the sentence.

The sun shone down on the icy landscape. <u>The sun</u> soon melted the snow so we were finally able to drive to school.

Pronoun: _____

1 mark

Pronouns and Possessive Pronouns

5 Which pair of **pronouns** completes the sentences below? Tick **one** box.

_____I_____ gave Mum a huge bunch of flowers. ___she___ was really pleased.

Tick **one**.

We, They ☐

He, You ☐

I, She ☑

We, We ☐

1 mark

6 Complete the passage below by adding suitable **possessive pronouns**.

The cakes I bought at the fair were _____. Cara thought they

were _____ but I knew _____ had cherries on

the top.

1 mark

Total marks .... /6   How am I doing? ☺ 😐 ☹

7

Determiners

1 Circle **all** the **determiners** in the sentence below.

After (a) big dinner, we ate (some fruit) with (a) scoop of ice-cream.

1 mark

2 Insert the missing **determiners** in the sentences below.

Stella put ___a___ letter in ___the___ envelope and put it in

___the___ post box.

Yesterday, at ___the___ zoo, we saw ___a___ monkey and

___an___ elephant.

1 mark

3 Circle **all** the **determiners** in the sentence below.

We enjoyed an evening of board games, a singing competition and a
delicious supper.

1 mark

4 Match the **determiner** on the left to the noun on the right.

the		orange
an		boys
some		pencil

1 mark

Determiners

5 Circle the **possessive determiner** in each sentence below.

We watched as our big brother raced around the park.

The cat has drunk its milk.

The fire fighters helped to rescue my dog.

1 mark

6 Which pair of **determiners** is missing from the sentence below?
Tick **one** box.

After _____ afternoon of sunshine, we were disappointed to see

_____ rain arrive.

Tick **one**.

a, an ☐

the, a ☐

an, the ☐

an, a ☐

1 mark

Total marks .... /6   How am I doing?

Prepositions

1   Tick **all** the sentences below that contain a **preposition**.

It's best to leave for the bus before 8:00am. ☐

After we left the cinema, we went home. ☐

Mum wrote her appointment time on the calendar. ☐

We found a little bird under the tree. ☐

1 mark

2   Circle the **two prepositions** in the sentence below.

During lunch time, we practised our spellings in the classroom.

1 mark

3   Insert suitable **prepositions** in the sentence below.

We looked _____ the table and _____ the door yet we still couldn't find our new kitten.

1 mark

4   Insert suitable **prepositions** in the sentences below.

After a long wait, we were finally able to go _____ the stadium.

The players ran _____ the pitch then lined up _____ the middle for the national anthem.

1 mark

Prepositions

5 Tick one box in each row below to indicate whether the word <u>after</u> in each sentence is used as a **preposition** or as a **subordinating conjunction**.

Sentence	<u>after</u> as a preposition	<u>after</u> as a subordinating conjunction
Freddy and I went home <u>after</u> the game had finished.		
Mum was pleased that I had cleaned the kitchen <u>after</u> the party.		

1 mark

6 Circle all the **prepositions** in the sentence below.

Our dog Monty dug a hole in the garden then hid behind the shed!

1 mark

7 Tick one box in each row below to indicate whether the word <u>until</u> in each sentence is used as a **preposition** or a **subordinating conjunction**.

Sentence	<u>until</u> used as a **preposition**	<u>until</u> used a **subordinating conjunction**
We played in the snow <u>until</u> we couldn't bear the cold.		
On holiday, Dad said we could stay up <u>until</u> 9:00pm.		

1 mark

Total marks .... /7   How am I doing? 😊 😐 😣

11

Adverbs and Adverbials

1 Circle the **adverbs** in each sentence below.

We often play tennis in the holidays.

The train arrived late so my parents missed the start of the film.

1 mark

2 Which word in the sentence below tells you **how** the baby drank his milk? Tick **one** box.

The baby's eyes began to close as he hungrily drank his milk.

1 mark

3 Rewrite the sentence below so that it starts with the **adverbial phrase**. Use only the same words, and remember to punctuate your answer correctly.

The astronauts contacted Earth after a successful launch.

_____

_____

_____

1 mark

4 Underline the **adverbials** in each sentence below.

My friend Zainab went skiing last week.

We decided that we would sail our boat towards the island.

1 mark

Adverbs and Adverbials

5 Tick **two** boxes to show the **adverbs** in the sentence below.

I still did not know whether it was best to be early for my audition or

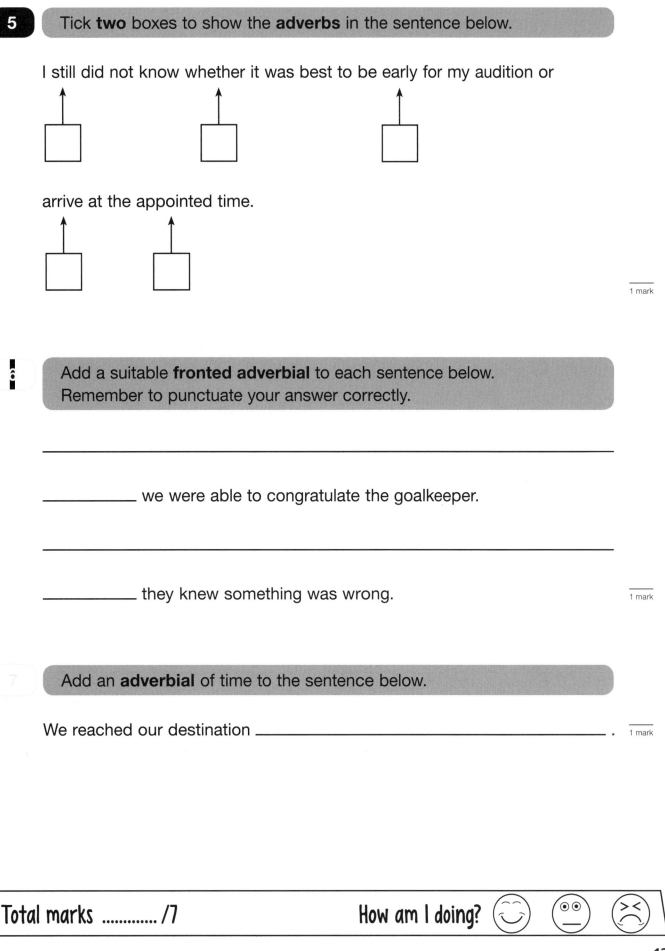

arrive at the appointed time.

1 mark

6 Add a suitable **fronted adverbial** to each sentence below.
Remember to punctuate your answer correctly.

_____

_____ we were able to congratulate the goalkeeper.

_____

_____ they knew something was wrong.

1 mark

7 Add an **adverbial** of time to the sentence below.

We reached our destination _____ . 1 mark

Total marks .... /7   How am I doing? 😊 😐 😣

Modal Verbs

1 Circle the **modal verb** that indicates **possibility** in the sentence below.

Dad said he might start training for the London Marathon.

1 mark

2 Choose a suitable **modal verb** to complete the sentence below.

Erin said, "I _____ walk the dog."

1 mark

Tick **one** box in each row below to show how the **modal verb** affects the meaning of the sentence.

Sentence	Modal verb indicates **possibility**.	Modal verb indicates **certainty**.
We might be able to pick you up on our way to school.		
The bus will come in ten minutes.		
Mum may let me stay up late tonight.		
My brother can dive from the top diving board!		

1 mark

4 Explain how the **modal verb** changes the meaning in each sentence below.

We will go swimming if it doesn't rain.

_____

_____

Modal Verbs

We could go swimming if it doesn't rain.

_____

_____ 1 mark

5 | Tick the **two** sentences below that indicate **possibility**.

Tick **two**.

Mum said I could play outside if I tidied my room. ☐

My brother will wash the dishes. ☐

Ted might help Dad mow the lawn. ☐

I can do handstands. ☐ 1 mark

6 | Insert a **modal verb** in the sentence below to indicate **possibility**.

According to the forecast, it _____ snow tomorrow. 1 mark

7 | Insert a **modal verb** in the sentence below to indicate **certainty**.

My friend Maria _____ speak two languages. 1 mark

Total marks .... /7   How am I doing? 😊 😐 😣

Subject and Object and Subject-Verb Agreement

1 What is the **subject** of the sentence below doing?

My grandma is baking cakes.

_____ 1 mark

2 Circle the **object** in the sentence below.

We couldn't stop staring at the excellent dancers. 1 mark

3 Label the boxes with **V (verb)**, **S (subject)** and **O (object)** to show the parts of the sentence.

My dog buried the bone.

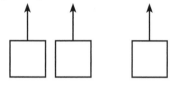

1 mark

4 Which **verb** agrees with the **subject** in the sentence below?
Tick **one** box.

Last weekend, we _____ DVDs with Dad.

Tick **one**.

watching ☐

watch ☐

watched ☐

watches ☐

1 mark

Subject and Object and Subject-Verb Agreement

5 Tick **one** box in each row below to indicate whether the words in bold in each sentence are the **subject** or the **object**.

Sentence	Subject	Object
The teacher handed out **the test papers**.		
The busy birds were building **nests**.		
We walked up to the top of the hill.		
Milo likes riding his bike.		

1 mark

6 Tick the **two** sentences where there is **subject–verb agreement**.

Tick **two**.

The naughty puppy were rolling in the long grass. ☐

We ate soup and crusty bread for our lunch. ☐

The wild wind will blowing all through the night. ☐

I made a chocolate cake for Mum's birthday. ☐

1 mark

Total marks .... /6   How am I doing?

Conjunctions and Relative Pronouns

1 Circle the **conjunction** in the sentence below.

Although it was late, we were allowed to stay up to watch the fireworks.

1 mark

2 Circle all the **conjunctions** in the sentences below.

The dentist said I should brush my teeth more often if I wanted healthy gums.

Once we were home, I spent ten minutes brushing carefully.

1 mark

3 Tick **one** box in each row below to indicate whether each underlined word is a **subordinating conjunction** or a **coordinating conjunction**.

Sentence	Subordinating conjunction	Coordinating conjunction
I like adventure <u>and</u> mystery films best.		
For dessert, we were allowed fruit <u>but</u> not ice-cream.		
<u>After</u> I finished my homework, I played outside.		
The brave boy played on, <u>even though</u> he had hurt his ankle.		

1 mark

4 Circle the **relative clause** in the sentence below.

The book that I read last month told the story of a magic unicorn.

1 mark

Conjunctions and Relative Pronouns

5 Tick the most suitable **conjunction** to complete the sentence below.

We put on our coats _____ we wanted to play in the garden.

Tick **one**.

although ☐

but ☐

as ☐

before ☐

1 mark

6 Insert a **relative pronoun** to complete the sentence below.

Our teacher, _____ house is in the countryside, was snowed in.

1 mark

7 Tick **one** box in each row below to indicate whether the words in bold are a **main clause** or a **subordinate clause**.

Sentence	Main clause	Subordinate clause
My brother, **who is mad about music**, went to see his favourite group.		
Our teacher was annoyed **because we didn't listen to her instructions**.		
Despite the fact that we weren't very hungry, **we still managed to eat a huge dinner**.		

1 mark

Total marks .... /7   How am I doing? 😊 😐 😣

Active and Passive Voice

1 Which sentence below is written in the **active voice**?

Tick **one**.

The cat was rescued by the firemen. ☐

The snow fell all through the night. ☐

Our garage roof was damaged by the storm. ☐

After a long chase, the robber was caught. ☐

1 mark

2 Rewrite the sentence below so that it is written in the **passive voice**. Remember to punctuate your answer correctly.

My parents won the holiday prize.

_____

_____

1 mark

3 Rewrite the sentence below so that it is written in the **active voice**. Remember to punctuate your answer correctly.

The fire-damaged building was rebuilt by a group of volunteers.

_____

_____

1 mark

Active and Passive Voice

4 Which sentence below is written in the **passive voice**?

Tick **one**.

We were fast asleep by the time the plane took off. ☐

The dogs were taken for a good long walk. ☐

Without a care in the world, Sami ran to the beach. ☐

When we got to the party, the cake was gone! ☐

1 mark

5 Say whether each sentence below is written in the **active** or **passive voice**.

The heavy rainfall flooded the farmer's fields.

_____

The farmer's fields were flooded by the heavy rainfall.

_____

Explain how you know.

_____

_____

_____

1 mark

Total marks .... /5   How am I doing? 🙂 😐 😣

Expanded Noun Phrases

1 Circle the **expanded noun phrase** in the sentence below.

My naughty brother spilled milk all over the table.

1 mark

2 Tick the sentence below that contains an **expanded noun phrase**.

Tick **one**.

At the funfair, we went on the dodgems and the slide. ☐

My mum bakes the best brownies in the world! ☐

We are going to Spain in the summer. ☐

Our teacher said we had behaved brilliantly on the trip. ☐

1 mark

3 Underline the longest possible **expanded noun phrase** in each sentence below.

Our long-awaited holiday to the seaside was ruined by the bad weather.

My brother's high-tech racing bike cost him a lot of money.

1 mark

Expanded Noun Phrases

4   Underline the **three expanded noun phrases** in the sentence below.

After a very long journey, the exhausted hockey team decided they would

stay in the hotel with luxury facilities and return home later.

1 mark

5   Make **expanded noun phrases** from the nouns on the left. An example has been done for you.

Noun	Expanded noun phrase
apples	some juicy, red apples
sea	
car	
children	
flowers	

1 mark

Total marks .... /5   How am I doing? 😊 😐 😣

Sentence Types

1 Tick the sentence below that must end with a **question mark**.

Tick **one**.

I asked the teacher a question about the homework ☐

It's quite cold outside, isn't it ☐

What an amazing surprise it was ☐

It's been such a long time since I've seen you ☐

1 mark

2 Tick the sentence below that is a **command**.

Tick **one**.

There are a few jobs I'd like you to do for me today. ☐

You have to work hard to get good results! ☐

Please put your name at the top of the page. ☐

Don't you need to take the dog for a walk? ☐

1 mark

Write a **question** below that ends with the following answer.

Question	Answer
	About 3 miles down the road.

1 mark

Sentence Types

4   Tick the sentence below that is a **statement.**

Tick **one.**

Start at the top of the page. ☐

Will you be going to the bank today? ☐

Remember to write a thank you note to Gran. ☐

Insects have six legs. ☐

1 mark

5   Underline the **imperative** verb in the command below.

Follow the recipe and you will produce a really great cake.

1 mark

6   Tick the **two** sentences below that must end with an **exclamation mark.**

Tick **two.**

You need to tidy up now ☐

What a big dog that is ☐

How wonderful to see you ☐

How many times have I told you ☐

1 mark

Total marks .... /6   How am I doing? ☺ 😐 ☹

Verb Tenses 1

1 Which pair of **verbs** completes the sentence below?

Last year, we _____ complaining about the cold and now we _____ moaning about the heat!

Tick **one**.

were, was	☐
was, is	☐
were, are	☐
are, are	☐

1 mark

2 Tick the sentence below that uses the **past progressive** tense.

Tick **one**.

Saida was working really hard to learn her times tables. ☐

My brother was quite ill over the holidays. ☐

We were sure that we had taken the right turning. ☐

No doubt it was the dog that chewed Dad's slippers. ☐

1 mark

Verb Tenses I

Tick the sentence below that uses the **present perfect** form of the verb.

Tick **one**.

Matt has worked hard this year. ☐

My sister is in a grumpy mood today. ☐

They are being very helpful to their parents. ☐

You are getting a lift to school tomorrow. ☐

1 mark

Tick **one** box in each row below to show if the sentence is in the **present progressive** or the **past progressive** tense.

Sentence	Present progressive	Past progressive
We were hoping for better weather than this.		
My friend is bringing me an ice-cream.		
The dogs are wagging their tails.		

1 mark

Rewrite the sentence below, changing the **present progressive verb** to the **past progressive**.

Our parents are watching a good documentary.

_____

_____

1 mark

Total marks .... /5   How am I doing? 😊 😐 😣

Verb Tenses 2

1 Circle the **present perfect form** of the verb in each sentence below.

After we **have taken / take** the cat to the vet, we will go for lunch.

She **has practised / is practising** her spellings all morning.

There **have been / were** worse storms than this one.

1 mark

2 Write the **present progressive** form of each verb in bold in the sentences below. An example has been done for you.

| are eating |

We **eat** our breakfast quickly so we don't miss the bus.

| |

The duckling **waddles** towards the river bank.

| |

I **think** of my poor, sick Grandad every day.

1 mark

3 Rewrite the sentences below so that they are in the **simple present** tense.

We played for hours with our new puppy. She drank milk and ate dried biscuits.

_____

_____

1 mark

Answers

Question	Requirement	Marks
	Pages 4–5 Word Classes – Nouns, Adjectives, Adverbs and Verbs	
1	My sister was very **apologetic** after she spilled water on my painting.	1
2	Answers will vary. Examples: The teacher switched the light on. (noun) Dad started to light the bonfire. (verb)	1
3	Our new kitten slept peacefully through the night. C (new) A (kitten) D (slept) B (night)	1
4	**Sentence** — Adjective / Adverb The car drove very <u>fast</u> round the corner. (Adverb ✓) We approached the tunnel's <u>wide</u> opening. (Adjective ✓) Maddie is wearing the <u>wrong</u> shoes! (Adjective ✓) We arrived <u>early</u> for the show. (Adverb ✓)	1
5	Correct insertion of **one** appropriate adverb, e.g. quickly, yesterday, well.	1
6	Sam was (possibly) going to arrive (late).	1
	Pages 6–7 Pronouns and Possessive Pronouns	
1	(I) walked to school because the bus didn't arrive.	1
2	Please give me those books back – they are **mine!**	1
3	My brother told **me** to hurry up. Our teacher explained the method to Mia and **me.** It was raining when Dan and **I** finally went into the playground. Mum and **I** finished eating then went for a walk.	1
4	The sun shone down on the icy landscape. **It** soon melted the snow so we were finally able to drive to school.	1
5	I, She ✓	1
6	Answers may vary. Example: The cakes I bought at the fair were **mine**. Cara thought they were **hers** but I knew **mine** had cherries on the top.	1
	Pages 8–9 Determiners	
1	After (a) big dinner, we ate (some) fruit with (a) scoop of ice-cream.	1
2	Stella put **a/the** letter in **an/the** envelope and put it in **a/the** post box. Yesterday, at **the/a** zoo, we saw **a/the** monkey and **an/the** elephant.	1
3	We enjoyed (an) evening of board games, (a) singing competition and (a) delicious supper.	1
4	an orange, some boys, the pencil	1
5	We watched as (our) brother raced around the park. The cat has drunk (its) milk. The fire fighters helped to rescue (my) dog.	1
6	an, the ✓	1
	Pages 10–11 Prepositions	
1	It's best to leave for the bus before 8:00am. ✓ Mum wrote her appointment time on the calendar. ✓ We found a little bird under the tree. ✓	1

1

2	(During) lunch time, we practised our spellings (in) the classroom.	1
3	Answers will vary. Examples: We looked **under/beneath/below** the table and **behind** the door yet we still couldn't find our new kitten.	1
4	Answers will vary. Examples: **into**; **onto/across/over/along**; **in/around**	1
5	Freddy and I went home after the game had finished. <u>after</u> as a **subordinating conjunction**. Mum was pleased that I had cleaned the kitchen after the party. <u>after</u> as a **preposition**.	1
6	Our dog Monty dug a hole (in) the garden then hid (behind) the shed!	1
7	We played in the snow <u>until</u> we couldn't bear the cold. <u>until</u> used as a **subordinating conjunction**. On holiday, Dad said we could stay up <u>until</u> 9:00pm. <u>until</u> used as a **preposition**.	1

Pages 12–13 Adverbs and Adverbials

1	We (often) play tennis in the holidays. The train arrived (late) so my parents missed the start of the film.	1
2	The baby's eyes began to close as he hungrily drank his milk. ↑ ✓	1
3	After a successful launch, the astronauts contacted Earth. *There must be a comma after the fronted adverbial.*	1
4	My friend Zainab went skiing <u>last week</u>. We decided that we would sail our boat <u>towards the island</u>.	1
5	I still did not know whether it was best to be early for my audition or arrive at the appointed time. ↑ ↑ ✓ ✓	1
6	Answers will vary. Sentence must start with a capital letter. Fronted adverbial must be followed by a comma. Examples: **After a long wait**, we were able to congratulate the goalkeeper. **At last**, we were able to congratulate the goalkeeper. **Immediately**, they knew something was wrong. **After a few minutes**, they knew something was wrong.	1
7	Answers will vary. Example: We reached our destination **late last night**.	1

Pages 14–15 Modal Verbs

1	Dad said he (might) start training for the London Marathon.	1
2	Erin said, "I **can/could/should/will/might/ought to** walk the dog."	1

3		Modal verb indicates **possibility**	Modal verb indicates **certainty**	1
	We might be able to pick you up on our way to school.	✓		
	The bus will come in ten minutes.		✓	
	Mum may let me stay up late tonight.	✓		
	My brother can dive from the top diving board!		✓	

4	In the first sentence, an answer that demonstrates understanding of the certainty of going swimming if it doesn't rain. In the second sentence, an answer that demonstrates understanding of the possibility of going swimming if it doesn't rain.	1
5	Mum said I could play outside if I tidied my room. ✓ Ted might help Dad mow the lawn. ✓	1
6	According to the forecast, it **might/may/could/should/ought to** snow tomorrow.	1
7	My friend Maria **can** speak two languages.	1

Pages 16–17 Subject and Object and Subject-Verb Agreement

1	baking/baking cakes	1
2	We couldn't stop staring at the excellent (dancers) *Also accept 'the excellent dancers' circled.*	1

3	My dog buried the bone. S V O	1
4	watched ✓	1

5		Subject	Object	1
	The teacher handed out **the test papers.**		✓	
	The busy birds were building **nests**.		✓	
	We walked up to the top of the hill.	✓		
	Milo likes riding his bike.	✓		

6	We ate soup and crusty bread for our lunch. ✓ I made a chocolate cake for Mum's birthday. ✓	1

Pages 18–19 Conjunctions and Relative Pronouns

1	(Although) it was late, we were allowed to stay up to watch the fireworks.	1
2	The dentist said I should brush my teeth more often (if) I wanted healthy gums. (Once) we were home, I spent ten minutes brushing carefully.	1

3		Subordinating	Coordinating	1
	I like adventure <u>and</u> mystery films best.		✓	
	For dessert, we were allowed fruit <u>but</u> not ice-cream.		✓	
	<u>After</u> I finished my homework, I played outside.	✓		
	The brave boy played on, <u>even though</u> he had hurt his ankle.	✓		

4	The book (that I read last month) told the story of a magic unicorn.	1
5	as ✓	1
6	Our teacher, **whose** house is in the countryside, was snowed in.	1

7		Main clause	Subordinate clause	1
	My brother, **who is mad about music,** went to see his favourite group.		✓	
	Our teacher was annoyed **because we didn't listen to her instructions**.		✓	
	Despite the fact that we weren't very hungry, **we still managed to eat a huge dinner**.	✓		

Pages 20–21 Active and Passive Voice

1	The snow fell all through the night. ✓	1
2	The holiday prize was won by my parents.	1
3	A group of volunteers rebuilt the fire-damaged building.	1
4	The dogs were taken for a good long walk. ✓	1
5	The heavy rainfall flooded the farmer's fields. **Active voice** The farmer's fields were flooded by the heavy rainfall. **Passive voice**. Explain how you know. Accept answers that show understanding that in the active voice sentence, the subject 'The heavy rainfall' is doing the action, and in the passive voice sentence, the subject 'The farmer's fields' are having the action 'done' to them.	1

Pages 22–23 Expanded Noun Phrases

1	(My naughty brother) spilled milk all over the table.	1
2	My mum bakes (the best brownies in the world.)	1
3	<u>Our long-awaited holiday to the seaside</u> was ruined by the bad weather. <u>My brother's high-tech racing bike</u> cost him a lot of money.	1
4	After <u>a very long journey</u>, <u>the exhausted hockey team</u> decided they would stay in <u>the hotel with luxury facilities</u> and return home later.	1

5	Answers will vary. As a minimum, noun should be modified by an adjective. Examples: the sparkling sea, my new car, those naughty children, some beautiful flowers	1
	Pages 24–25 Sentence Types	
1	It's quite cold outside, isn't it ✓	1
2	Please put your name at the top of the page. ✓	1
3	Answers will vary. Example: Where is the post office? Questions must start with a capital letter and end with a question mark for the mark to be awarded.	1
4	Insects have six legs. ✓	1
5	<u>Follow</u> the recipe and you will produce a really great cake.	1
6	What a big dog that is ✓ How wonderful to see you ✓	1
	Pages 26–27 Verb Tenses 1	
1	were, are ✓	1
2	Saida was working really hard to learn her times tables. ✓	1
3	Matt has worked hard this year. ✓	1
4	<table><tr><td>Sentence</td><td>**Present progressive**</td><td>**Past progressive**</td></tr><tr><td>We were hoping for better weather than this.</td><td></td><td>✓</td></tr><tr><td>My friend is bringing me an ice-cream.</td><td>✓</td><td></td></tr><tr><td>The dogs are wagging their tails.</td><td>✓</td><td></td></tr></table>	1
5	Our parents were watching a good documentary.	1
	Pages 28–29 Verb Tenses 2	
1	After we (have taken) the cat to the vet, we will go for lunch. She (has practised) her spellings all morning. There (have been) worse storms than this one.	1
2	The duckling **is waddling** towards the river bank. I **am thinking** of my poor, sick Grandad every day.	1
3	We play for hours with our new puppy. She drinks milk and eats dried biscuits.	1
4	have jumped **had jumped** **have fallen** had fallen have been **had been** **have written** had written	1
5	After we **have eaten** our sandwiches, we will go for a walk. There **has been** a burglary in the night.	1
6	I **went** further into the dark cave until I **came** to a pool of shimmering water. For a moment, I **thought** about turning back but I **felt** a stronger urge to continue.	1
	Pages 30–31 Progress Test 1	
1	**It** is usually warm and sunny but in case **it** is wet and windy, **I/we** will take waterproofs.	1
2	Answers will vary. Examples: The roads were flooded because it had rained heavily. Answers that begin with the subordinate clause must be followed by a comma: After it had rained heavily, the roads were flooded.	1
3	a verb ✓	1
4	We could have watched <u>the dancers in their sparkly dresses</u> all night.	1
5	Active voice.	1

6	<u>Our neighbour's shed, which he kept locked, was broken into last night.</u>
	                          ↑
	                          ✓
		1

7	After an exhausting eight-hour journey, we were all desperate to go to bed. *The fronted adverbial must be followed by a comma.*	1
8	We found the key (under) a tree. We inserted it (into) the lock (in) the old wooden box and turned it.	1
9	<u>The</u> main act entered <u>the</u> ring. There was <u>an</u> acrobat, <u>a</u> lion and <u>some</u> clowns.	1
Pages 32–33 Full Stops, Capital Letters, Exclamation and Question Marks		
1	It's almost time for bed, isn't it? ✓	1
2	Accept answers that state they are all proper nouns. Or: They are the names of a place, a country and a person. Do not accept 'nouns'.	1
3	<u>on</u> <u>wednesday</u>, <u>mr burrows</u> told us about the first astronauts in space. <u>we</u> looked at pictures of the <u>earth</u> and we could make out the <u>atlantic ocean</u> and the continent of <u>africa</u>.	1
4	It's a bit late to start watching a film, isn't it?	1
5	exclamation mark ✓	1
6	Due to the unusually hot summer, we were allowed to bring water bottles to school. The head teacher, Mrs Stephens, even provided fans in the classrooms. What a relief it was!	1
7	In August, we will drive to Italy for a holiday.	1
Pages 34–35 Brackets, Dashes and Commas		
1	After our long sleep, we woke up feeling refreshed. ✓	1
2	Daffodils are usually associated with spring they are bright yellow flowers with long, straight leaves. ↑ ✓	1
3	Accept answers that show understanding that the second sentence suggests that *all* fruit and vegetables are fresh and organic, whereas the first sentence suggests that only fruit and vegetables which are fresh and organic are the healthiest food choice.	1
4	My grandmother (who only last year suffered a broken ankle) has just completed the London Marathon.	1
5	My gran's cat – which is called Sheba – likes to drink cream. OR My gran's cat, which is called Sheba, likes to drink cream.	1
6	My big brother Miles, a rugby fanatic, travels all over the country to watch his favourite team.	1
7	Louie – always keen to be the first – fell over in his rush to the playground.	1
Pages 36–37 Inverted Commas		
1	"I want you to close your books now, please," instructed our teacher. ✓	1
2	"Would you like to go to the park?" they asked. Or: They asked, "Would you like to go to the park?"	1
3	"I have decided to take you all to watch the cycling at the velodrome," announced Dad.	1
4	Ryan asked, "You are coming out to play, aren't you?" ✓	1
5	Martha asked her mum if it was time to leave for the airport. "Not just yet," said Mum. "We have plenty of time. We don't want to get there too early." "That's true," Martha agreed. "The flight isn't until 2 o'clock."	1
6	"There will be showers most of the day with temperatures staying mild,'' the weather forecaster said.	1
Pages 38–39 Apostrophes to Show Possession		
1	To show that the trainer belongs to Michael. ✓	1
2	The dog's owners apologised when it licked my face. ✓	1

3	the child's artwork, the children's artwork, the ladies' scarves, the lady's scarf	1
4	My dentist's chair isn't very comfortable! ✓	1

Pages 40–41 Apostrophes to Show Contraction

1	To contract the words *there* and *has*. ✓	1
2	I had – I'd, did not – didn't, should not – shouldn't, could have – could've, shall not – shan't, they would – they'd	1
3	they had, they would, would not	1
4	haven't	1
5	After they finish this race, they'll know if they're the winners. ✓	1
6	**We've** been waiting for the bus to come for ages but **it's** nowhere to be seen.	1

Pages 42–43 Semi-colons, Colons, Commas, Hyphens and Bullet Points

1	colon ✓	1
2	Mum and I love watching live football; my brother and Dad, however, prefer watching it on the TV.	1
3	Our teachers asked us to set up the classroom for the art lesson: paints, water, brushes and paper were all required.	1
4	For our school trip tomorrow, we are bringing packed lunches, water bottles, waterproof coats, cameras and binoculars.	1
5	My auntie Marla wears only up-to-date designer clothes. ✓	1
6	<ul><li>bread</li><li>knife</li><li>toaster or grill</li><li>plate</li><li>butter</li><li>jam</li></ul>	1
7	My mum likes to drink sugar-free tea and coffee.	1

Pages 44–45 Progress Test 2

1	My brother, though annoying at times, brings so much fun to our family.	1
2	My baby sister's first tooth has appeared! ✓	1
3	Those boys are playing tennis.	1
4	Claire said it wasn't my pencil, it was **hers**, because **mine/hers** was pink whereas **hers/mine** was green.	1
5	an adverb ✓	1
6	We thought a safari would be a great idea for our summer holiday. Dad did lots of research on the internet and he finally settled on South Africa. He has booked it for December as the weather will be warm and sunny then. What an exciting trip to look forward to!	1
7	"The motorway will be blocked for two hours," said the TV news reader. Or: The TV news reader said, "The motorway will be blocked for two hours."	1
8	Even though it's raining, let's play outside.	1

Pages 46–47 Synonyms and Antonyms

1	annoy ✓	1
2	discover/uncover, illegible, impractical, irresponsible	1
3	weary, tired	1
4	cowardly – courageous, enemy – ally, opaque – transparent, rigid – flexible	1
5	roomy ✓	1

	Pages 48–49 Root Words and Word Families	
1	self ✓	1
2	at a distance ✓	1
3	geology, hemisphere, autograph, bisect	1
4	Answers may vary. Examples: construct, destruct, instruct	1
5	write ✓	1
	Pages 50–51 Adding Suffixes	
1	fearful/fearless/fearsome, crazy, cautious, competitive	1
2	official, gracious, ambitious, confidential	1
3	appreciation, blockage, arrival, adjustment, insurance	1
4	brightness, flexibility, difficulty, clumsiness, ability	1
5	hopeful/hopeless, lovable/lovely, furious, cloudy/cloudless	1
	Pages 52–53 Formal, Informal and Standard English	
1	After our breakfast, we **feeled/felt** really full. My friend and I **was/were** excited about the performance.	1
2	When we were driving home, we saw a rabbit in the middle of the road. Mum said we would have gone to Spain on holiday but it was too expensive.	1
3	I wish I <u>were</u> a fly on the wall so I could see what was going on. She would sail around the Caribbean on a yacht if she <u>were</u> a millionaire.	1
4	Your personal diary entry: informal; A letter to the Head Teacher: formal; A postcard to your best friend: informal.	1
5		Formal	Informal		1
	We goin' to footie training tonight, Jaz?		✓		
	Ladies and gentlemen, I'd like to welcome you to our school production.	✓			
	Must get a pressie for Mum's birthday!		✓		
	Please accept my congratulations on your new job.	✓			
6	be ✓	1
7	If there **were** to be a fire, proceed to the emergency exit doors.	1
	Pages 54–56 Progress Test 3	
1	look or see ✓	1
2	would, must, might, should	1
3	misunderstand, illegal, impenetrable, inoperable	1
4	dullness, prettiness, desperation, caution/cautiousness, enjoyment	1
5	professional ✓	1
6	It was (a) lovely day so (the) family set off early in (the) morning.	
7	(Five baby chicks) waddled towards the water's edge.	1
8	fresh – new, unusual – strange, argue – squabble, guess – estimate, stick – adhere	1
9	(a) The old dog (the one with the sad brown eyes) limped slowly across the field. (b) Either: double dashes or a pair of commas. Accept dashes or commas.	1 / 1
10	Answers will vary. Example: If you can wait a second I'll / I will get my coat and come with you.	1

Progress Test Charts

Progress Test 1

Q	Topic	✓ or ✗	See Page
1	Pronouns		6
2	Conjunctions and Relative Pronouns		18
3	Word Classes		4
4	Expanded Noun Phrases		22
5	Active and Passive Voice		20
6	Conjunctions and Relative Pronouns		18
7	Adverbs and Adverbials		12
8	Prepositions		10
9	Determiners		8

Progress Test 2

Q	Topic	✓ or ✗	See Page
1	Brackets, Dashes and Commas		34
2	Apostrophes to Show Possession		38
3	Sentence Types		24
4	Pronouns		6
5	Word Classes		4
6	Full Stops, Capital Letters, Exclamation and Question Marks		32
7	Inverted Commas		36
8	Apostrophes to Show Contraction		40

Progress Test 3

Q	Topic	✓ or ✗	See Page
1	Root Words and Word Families		48
2	Modal Verbs		14
3	Root Words and Word Families		48
4	Adding Suffixes		50
5	Synonyms and Antonyms		46
6	Determiners		8
7	Subject and Object and Subject–Verb Agreement		16
8	Synonyms and Antonyms		46
9	Brackets, Dashes and Commas		34
10	Formal, Informal and Standard English		52

What am I doing well in?

_____

_____

What do I need to improve?

_____

_____

Verb Tenses 2

4 Complete the table below. An example has been done for you.

Present perfect	Past perfect
have broken	*had broken*
have jumped	
	had fallen
have been	
	had written

1 mark

5 Which **verb form** is correct in each of the sentences below? Circle **one**.

After we **had eaten / have eaten** our sandwiches, we will go for a walk.

There **has been / have been** a burglary in the night.

1 mark

6 Complete the sentences below using the **simple past** tense of the verbs in the boxes.

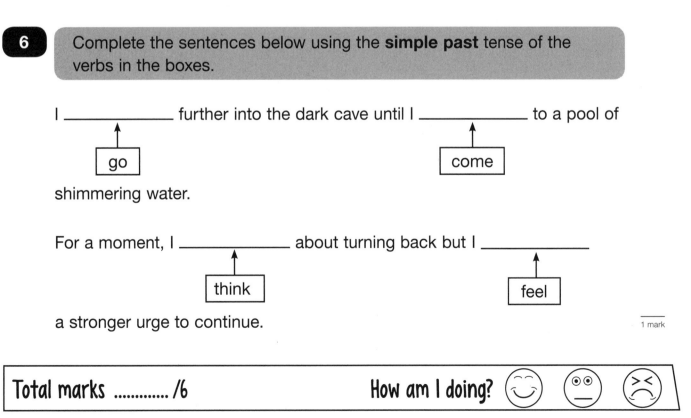

I _____ further into the dark cave until I _____ to a pool of

go

come

shimmering water.

For a moment, I _____ about turning back but I _____

think

feel

a stronger urge to continue.

1 mark

Total marks .... /6   How am I doing? 😊 😐 😣

29

Progress Test 1

1 Insert suitable **pronouns** in the short passage below.

Tomorrow, I am going to the seaside. _____ is usually warm and

sunny but in case _____ is wet and windy, _____ will take

waterproofs.

1 mark

2 Rewrite the sentence below adding a **subordinate clause**. Remember to punctuate your sentence correctly.

The roads were flooded.

_____

1 mark

3 What **word class** is <u>bark</u> in the sentence below? Tick **one** box.

My neighbour's dog likes to bark at people walking past.

Tick one.

a noun ☐

an adverb ☐

a verb ☐

a conjunction ☐

1 mark

4 Underline the **expanded noun phrase** in the sentence below.

We could have watched the dancers in their sparkly dresses all night.

1 mark

5 Is the sentence below written in the **active voice** or the **passive voice**?

We drove by the parliament building.

Answer: _____

1 mark

6 Tick **one** box to indicate which part of the sentence below is a **relative clause**.

Our neighbour's shed, which he kept locked, was broken into last night.

1 mark

7 Rewrite the sentence below so that it starts with the **adverbial**.

We were all desperate to go to bed after an exhausting eight-hour journey.

_____

_____

1 mark

8 Circle the **three prepositions** in the sentences below.

We found the key under a tree. We inserted it into the lock in the old

wooden box and turned it.

1 mark

9 Underline all the **determiners** in the sentences below.

The main act entered the ring. There was an acrobat, a lion and some clowns.

1 mark

Total marks .... /9   How am I doing?   ☺   😐   😣

31

Full Stops, Capital Letters, Exclamation and Question Marks

1 Which sentence below is correctly **punctuated**?

Tick **one**.

We're so pleased that Mrs smith has moved next door. ☐

my dad is going to London in the morning. ☐

It's almost time for bed, isn't it? ☐

"What an amazing sculpture that is" ☐

1 mark

2 Why do the words in bold in the sentence below begin with a **capital letter**?

We visited **Buckingham Palace** in **London, England**, which is the home of **Queen Elizabeth II.**

_____

_____

1 mark

3 Underline the words that should start with a **capital letter** in the passage below.

on wednesday, mr burrows told us about the first astronauts in space.
we looked at pictures of the earth and we could make out the atlantic
ocean and the continent of africa.

1 mark

4 Insert the missing punctuation mark in the sentence below.

It's a bit late to start watching a film, isn't it

1 mark

Full Stops, Capital Letters, Exclamation and Question Marks

5 Which **punctuation mark** should be inserted in the place indicated by the arrow? Tick **one** box.

"What an amazing story that was ↑ " gasped Milo as his teacher closed the book.

Tick **one**.

question mark ☐

comma ☐

full stop ☐

exclamation mark ☐

1 mark

6 Correct the **punctuation** in the following sentences. One has been done for you.

D

d̸ue to the unusually hot summer, we were allowed to bring water

bottles to school the head teacher, mrs stephens, even provided

fans in the classrooms what a relief it was

1 mark

7 Rewrite the sentence below, using correct **punctuation**.

in august, we will drive to italy for a holiday

_____ 1 mark

Total marks .... /7   How am I doing? 😊 😐 😣

Brackets, Dashes and Commas

1 Which sentence below has been **punctuated** correctly?

Tick **one**.

After, our long sleep we woke up feeling refreshed. ☐

After our long sleep, we woke up feeling refreshed. ☐

After our long, sleep we woke up, feeling refreshed. ☐

After our long sleep we woke up feeling, refreshed. ☐

1 mark

2 Tick **one** box to show where a **dash** should go in the sentence below.

Daffodils are usually associated with spring they are bright yellow flowers

☐↑ ☐↑ ☐↑

with long, straight leaves.

1 mark

3 Explain how the use of **commas** changes the meaning in each sentence below.

Fruit and vegetables which are fresh and organic are the healthiest food choice.

Fruit and vegetables, which are fresh and organic, are the healthiest food choice.

_____

_____

1 mark

Brackets, Dashes and Commas

4 Insert a pair of **brackets** in the sentence below.

My grandmother who only last year suffered a broken ankle has just completed the London Marathon.

1 mark

5 Rewrite the sentence below using a **different** pair of punctuation marks on either side of the words <u>which is called Sheba</u>.

My gran's cat (which is called Sheba) likes to drink cream.

_____

_____

1 mark

6 Insert a **pair of commas** to show **parenthesis** in the sentence below.

My big brother Miles a rugby fanatic travels all over the country to watch his favourite team.

1 mark

7 Rewrite the sentence below, inserting a pair of **dashes** in the correct place.

Louie always keen to be the first fell over in his rush to the playground.

_____

_____

1 mark

Total marks .... /7   How am I doing? ☺ 😐 ☹

Inverted Commas

1 Which sentence below uses **inverted commas** correctly?

Tick **one**.

"I want you to close your books now, please instructed our teacher." ☐

"I want you to close your books now," please instructed our teacher. ☐

"I want you to close your books now, please," instructed our teacher. ☐

"I want you to close your books now, please", instructed our teacher. ☐

1 mark

2 Rewrite the sentence below as **direct speech**. Remember to punctuate your answer correctly.

They asked if we would like to go to the park.

_____

_____

1 mark

3 Insert the missing **inverted commas** in the sentence below.

I have decided to take you all to watch the cycling at the velodrome, announced Dad.

1 mark

Inverted Commas

4 | Which sentence below is correctly punctuated with **inverted commas**?

Tick **one**.

Ryan asked, "You are coming out to play, aren't you?" ☐

Ryan asked You "are coming out to play, aren't you?" ☐

Ryan asked, "You are coming out to play," aren't you? ☐

Ryan asked, "You are coming out to play" aren't you? ☐

1 mark

5 | Add the missing **inverted commas** to the passage below.

Martha asked her mum if it was time to leave for the airport.

Not just yet, said Mum. We have plenty of time. We don't want to get there too early.

That's true, Martha agreed. The flight isn't until 2 o'clock.

1 mark

6 | Tick **two** boxes where the missing **inverted commas** should go.

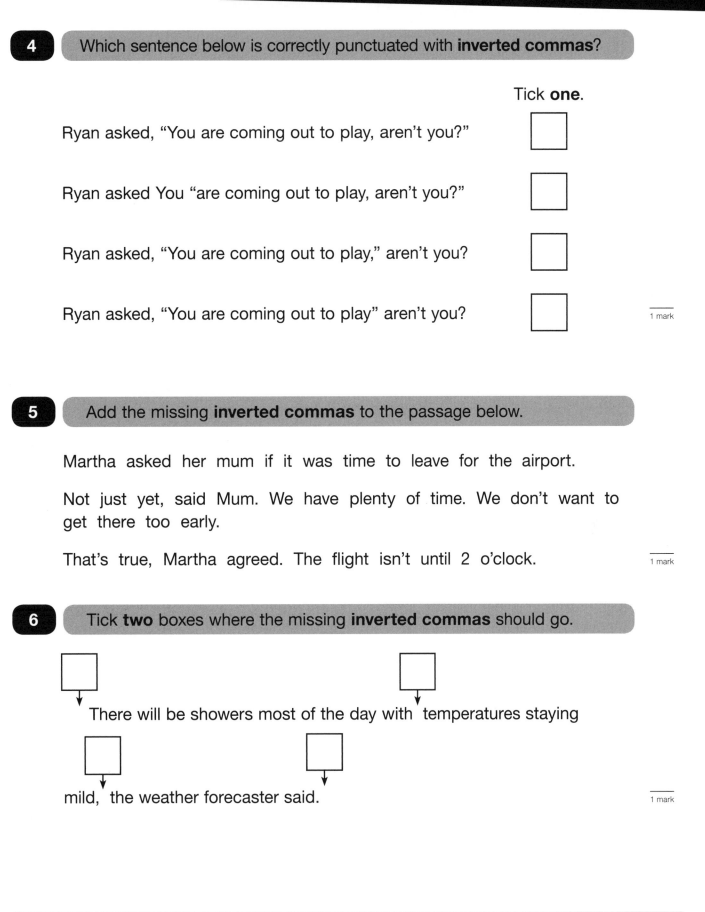

☐   ☐

There will be showers most of the day with temperatures staying

☐   ☐

mild, the weather forecaster said.

1 mark

Total marks .... /6   How am I doing? ☺ 😐 ☹

37

Apostrophes to Show Possession

1   Why has an **apostrophe** been used in the sentence below? Tick **one** box.

Michael's trainer fell off as he was running in the race!

Tick **one**.

To show that Michael belongs to the trainer. ☐

To show that the trainer belongs to Michael. ☐

To show that *Michael's* is a contraction. ☐

To show that something funny happened. ☐

1 mark

2   Which sentence below uses an **apostrophe** correctly?

Tick **one**.

The dogs' owners apologised when it licked my face. ☐

The dog's owners apologised when it licked my face. ☐

The dogs owner's apologised when it licked my face. ☐

The dogs owners' apologised when it licked my face. ☐

1 mark

Apostrophes to Show Possession

3 Write the following phrases so that they contain an **apostrophe to show possession**. One has been done for you.

the book belonging to my best friend	*my best friend's book*
the artwork belonging to the child	
the artwork belonging to the children	
the scarves belonging to the ladies	
the scarf belonging to the lady	

1 mark

4 Which sentence has been punctuated correctly with an **apostrophe**?

Tick **one**.

Our clothes' became soaked in the pouring rain. ☐

My dentist's chair isn't very comfortable! ☐

The dog chased it's tail. ☐

The younger classes' are allowed to go home early. ☐

1 mark

Total marks .... /4   How am I doing?

Apostrophes to Show Contraction

1 Why has an **apostrophe** been used in the sentence below?

There's been a lot of interest in our house since we put it up for sale.

Tick **one**.

To make it easier to say. ☐

To contract the words *there* and *has*. ☐

To show possession. ☐

To contract the words *there* and *is*. ☐

1 mark

2 Match the words on the left to their **contracted forms** on the right.

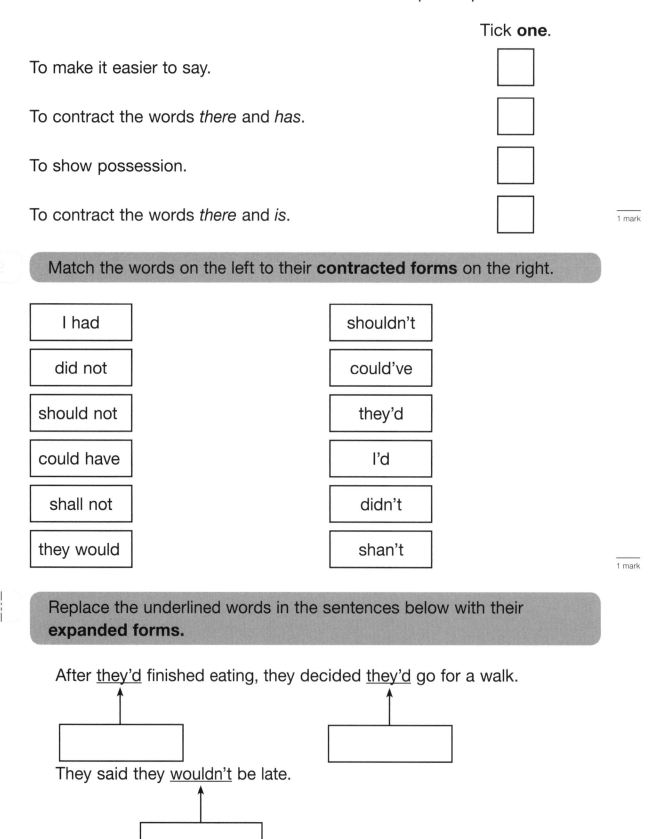

I had	shouldn't
did not	could've
should not	they'd
could have	I'd
shall not	didn't
they would	shan't

1 mark

3 Replace the underlined words in the sentences below with their **expanded forms.**

After <u>they'd</u> finished eating, they decided <u>they'd</u> go for a walk.

☐   ☐

They said they <u>wouldn't</u> be late.

☐

1 mark

40

Apostrophes to Show Contraction

4 Write the **contracted form** of the underlined words below in the box.

We <u>have not</u> been to London before.

1 mark

5 Which sentence below uses the correctly **contracted forms** of the words *they will* and *they are*?

Tick **one**.

After they finish this race, theyl'l know if theyr'e the winners.

After they finish this race, they'll know if they're the winners.

After they finish this race, theyll know if theyre the winners.

After they finish this race, the'yll know if the'yre the winners.

1 mark

6 **Contract** the underlined words in the sentence below using an **apostrophe**.

<u>We have</u> been waiting for the bus to come for ages but <u>it is</u> nowhere to be seen.

1 mark

Total marks .... /6   How am I doing?

Semi-colons, Colons, Commas, Hyphens and Bullet Points

1 Which **punctuation mark** should be used in the place indicated by the arrow? Tick **one** box.

There was a wide range of animals at the zoo↑ giraffes, monkeys, flamingos, walrus, kangaroos and alligators were just some of the ones we saw.

Tick **one**.

semi-colon ☐

comma ☐

full stop ☐

colon ☐

1 mark

2 Insert a **semi-colon** in the correct place in the sentence below.

Mum and I love watching live football my brother and Dad, however, prefer watching it on the TV.

1 mark

3 Insert a **colon** in the correct place in the sentence below.

Our teachers asked us to set up the classroom for the art lesson paints, water, brushes and paper were all required.

1 mark

Insert the missing **commas** in the correct places in the sentence below.

For our school trip tomorrow we are bringing packed lunches water bottles waterproof coats cameras and binoculars.

1 mark

Semi-colons, Colons, Commas, Hyphens and Bullet Points

5 Which sentence below uses the **hyphen** correctly?

Tick **one**.

My auntie Marla wears only up-to-date designer clothes. ☐

My auntie Marla wears only up to-date designer clothes. ☐

My auntie Marla wears only up to date designer-clothes. ☐

My auntie Marla wears only-up-to-date designer clothes. ☐

1 mark

6 Change the sentence below into a list using **bullet points**.

To make tasty toast, you will need bread, a knife, a toaster or grill, a plate, butter and jam.

To make tasty toast, you will need the following:

_____   _____

_____   _____

_____   _____

1 mark

7 Insert a **hyphen** in the correct position in the sentence below.

My mum likes to drink sugar free tea and coffee.

1 mark

Total marks .... /7   How am I doing? 😊 😐 😖

Progress Test 2

1 Insert a pair of **commas** to indicate **parenthesis** in the sentence below.

My brother though annoying at times brings so much fun to our family.

1 mark

2 Which sentence below uses an **apostrophe to show possession** correctly?

Tick **one**.

My baby sisters' first tooth has appeared! ☐

My baby sister's' first tooth has appeared! ☐

My baby sister's first tooth has appeared! ☐

My baby' sisters first tooth has appeared! ☐

1 mark

Rearrange the words in the question below to make it a **statement**. Remember to punctuate your sentence correctly and do not use any additional words.

Are those boys playing tennis?

_____

_____

1 mark

Insert suitable **possessive pronouns** into this sentence.

Claire said it wasn't my pencil, it was _____, because

_____ was pink whereas _____ was green.

1 mark

44

5   What **word class** is <u>yesterday</u> in the sentence below?

The two girls went for a long run yesterday.

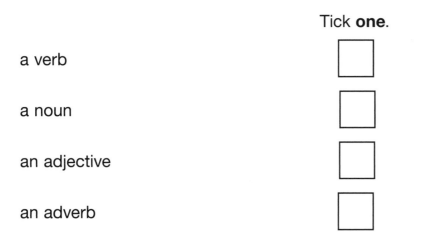

Tick **one**.

a verb ☐

a noun ☐

an adjective ☐

an adverb ☐

1 mark

6   **Punctuate** the following sentence correctly. The first one has been done for you.

W
~~w~~e thought a safari would be a great idea for our summer holiday dad did lots

of research on the internet and he finally settled on south africa he has booked it

for december as the weather will be warm and sunny then what an exciting trip to

look forward to

1 mark

7   Turn this sentence into **direct speech** using **inverted commas**.

The TV news reader said the motorway would be blocked for two hours.

_____

1 mark

8   Add the missing **two apostrophes** to the sentence below.

Even though its raining, lets play outside.

1 mark

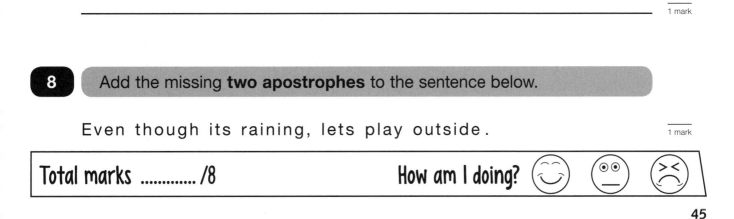

Total marks .... /8   How am I doing?

45

Synonyms and Antonyms

1 Which word is closest in meaning to <u>harass</u>?

Tick **one**.

annoy ☐

hurry ☐

finish ☐

persuade ☐

1 mark

2 Add a **prefix** to each word below to form its **antonym**.

_____ cover

_____ legible

_____ practical

_____ responsible

1 mark

3 Which two words in the sentence below are **synonyms** of each other?

Gran is weary after spending a whole day working in the garden; you can tell when she's tired as she gets a bit grumpy!

_____ and _____

1 mark

Synonyms and Antonyms

1 Draw a line to match each word to its correct **antonym**.

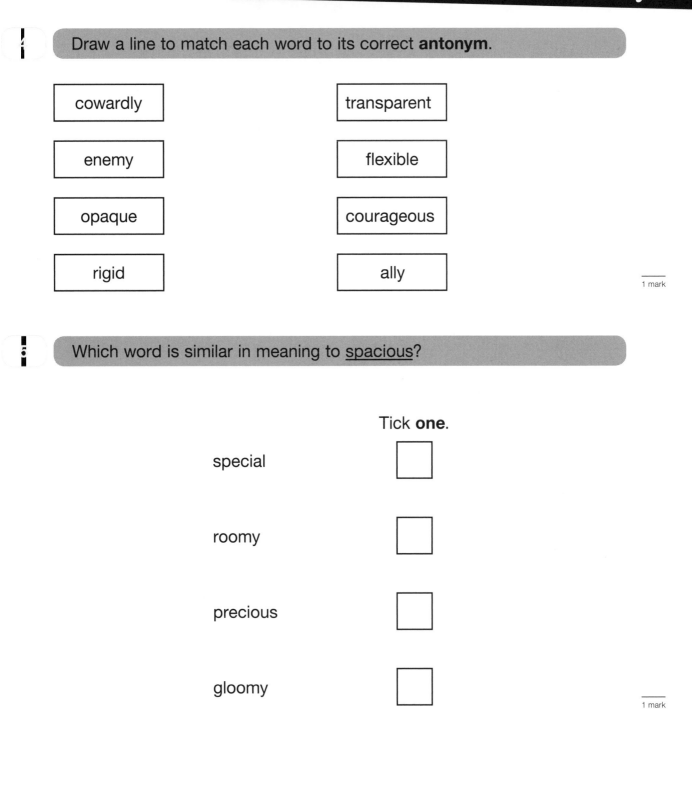

cowardly	transparent
enemy	flexible
opaque	courageous
rigid	ally

1 mark

2 Which word is similar in meaning to <u>spacious</u>?

Tick **one**.

special ☐

roomy ☐

precious ☐

gloomy ☐

1 mark

Total marks .... /5   How am I doing? 😊 😐 😖

Root Words and Word Families

1 What does the **prefix** 'auto' mean in this group of words?

automatic   **auto**biography   **auto**pilot   **auto**mobile

Tick **one**.

other ☐

separate ☐

self ☐

assist ☐

1 mark

2 What does the root 'tele' mean in the word family below?

telephone   **tele**scope   **tele**graph   **tele**vision

Tick **one**.

close up ☐

magnify ☐

minimise ☐

at a distance ☐

1 mark

Root Words and Word Families

3 Match each **prefix** to a **suffix** to form a complete word.

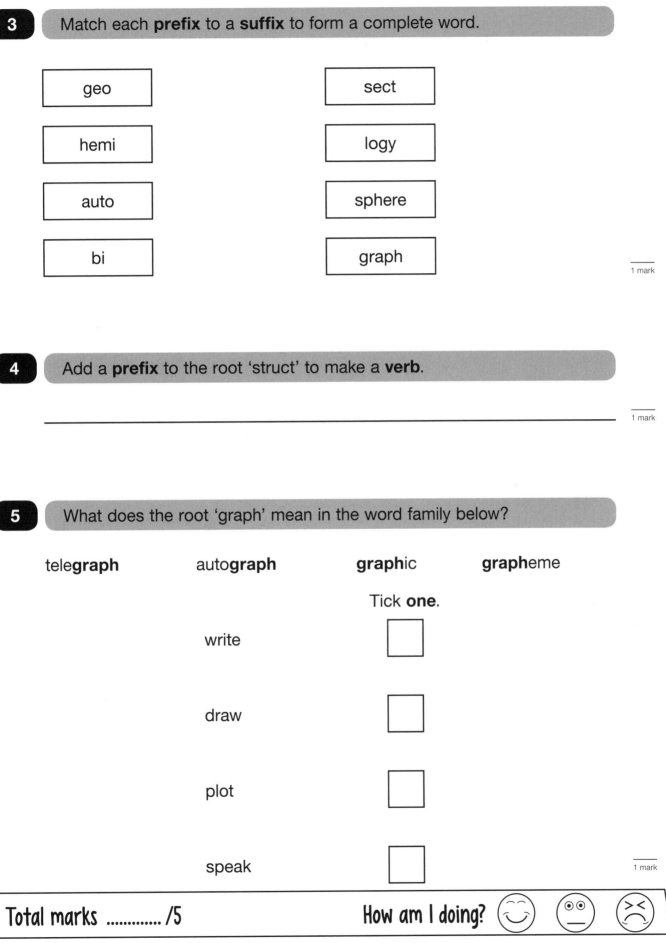

| geo |
| hemi |
| auto |
| bi |

| sect |
| logy |
| sphere |
| graph |

1 mark

4 Add a **prefix** to the root 'struct' to make a **verb**.

_____

1 mark

5 What does the root 'graph' mean in the word family below?

tele**graph**   auto**graph**   **graph**ic   **graph**eme

Tick **one**.

write ☐

draw ☐

plot ☐

speak ☐

1 mark

Total marks .... /5   How am I doing? ☺ 😐 ☹

Adding Suffixes

1   Add a **suffix** to each **noun** in the table below to make an **adjective**.

Noun	Adjective
fear	
craze	
caution	
competition	

1 mark

2   Choose either **ious**, **ial** or **tial** to change each noun below into an adjective.

office (noun) _____ (adjective)

grace (noun) _____ (adjective)

ambition (noun) _____ (adjective)

confidence (noun) _____ (adjective)

1 mark

3   Change each **verb** on the left into a **noun** by adding one of the
following **suffixes**.

ion   **ment**   **ance**   **age**   **al**

Verb	Noun
to appreciate	
to block	
to arrive	
to adjust	
to insure	

1 mark

Adding Suffixes

4 Complete the table below by adding a **suffix** to each **adjective** to make a **noun**.

Adjective	Noun
bright	
flexible	
difficult	
clumsy	
able	

1 mark

5 Complete the table below by adding a **suffix** to each **noun** to make an **adjective**.

Noun	Adjective
hope	
love	
fury	
cloud	

1 mark

Total marks .... /5   How am I doing? ☺ 😐 😣

Formal, Informal and Standard English

1 Circle **one verb** in each pair in bold to complete the sentences below using **Standard English**.

After our breakfast, we **feeled / felt** really full.

My friend and I **was / were** excited about the performance.

1 mark

2 Rewrite each sentence below in **Standard English.**

When we was driving home, we seen a rabbit in the middle of the road.

_____

_____

Mum said we would of gone to Spain on holiday but it were too expensive.

_____

_____

1 mark

3 Underline the verb that is in the **subjunctive mood** in each sentence below.

I wish I were a fly on the wall so I could see what was going on.

She would sail around the Caribbean on a yacht if she were a millionaire.

1 mark

4 Tick the correct box below to indicate whether the type of writing listed on the left is **formal** or **informal**.

Type of writing	Formal	Informal
Your personal diary entry		
A letter to the Head Teacher		
A postcard to your best friend		

1 mark

Formal, Informal and Standard English

5 Say whether each sentence below is **formal** or **informal**.

Sentence	Formal	Informal
We goin' to footie training tonight, Jaz?		
Ladies and gentlemen, I'd like to welcome you to our school production.		
Must get a pressie for Mum's birthday!		
Please accept my congratulations on your new job.		

1 mark

6 Which verb option below completes the sentence so that it is in the **subjunctive mood**? Tick **one** box.

The teacher asked that the younger pupils _____ quiet while the tests took place.

Tick **one**.

are ☐

went ☐

be ☐

were ☐

1 mark

7 Complete the sentence below so that it uses the **subjunctive form**.

If there _____ to be a fire, proceed to the emergency exit doors.

1 mark

Total marks .... /7   How am I doing? 😊 😐 😣

Progress Test 3

1 What does the root 'spect' mean in the word family below?

spectator   **spect**acle   **spect**acles   in**spect**

Tick **one**.

touch or feel ☐

look or see ☐

listen or hear ☐

write or draw ☐

1 mark

2 Circle the **modal verbs** in these sentences.

Tom would like to watch the football, but his mum said he must do his homework.

The cat might eat the tuna, so we should put it away.

1 mark

3 Add a **prefix** to each word to give it a **negative meaning**.

understand _____

legal   _____

penetrable _____

operable   _____

1 mark

4 Complete the table below by adding a **suffix** to each **adjective** to make a **noun**.

Adjective	Noun
dull	
pretty	
desperate	
cautious	
enjoy	

1 mark

5 Which word is an **antonym** of <u>amateur</u>?

Tick **one**.

celebrity ☐

professional ☐

doctor ☐

beginner ☐

1 mark

6 Circle all the **determiners** in the sentence below.

It was a lovely day so the family set off early in the morning.

1 mark

7 Circle the **subject** in the sentence below.

Five baby chicks waddled towards the water's edge.

1 mark

8 Draw a line to match each word on the left with its **synonym** on the right.

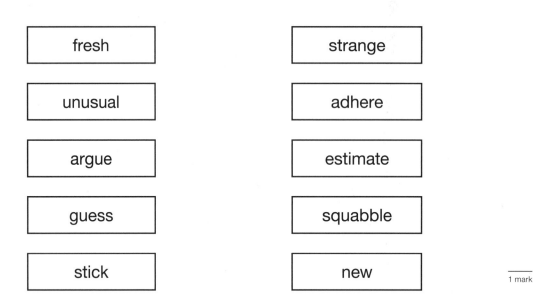

fresh	strange
unusual	adhere
argue	estimate
guess	squabble
stick	new

1 mark

9 (a) Insert a pair of brackets to show **parenthesis** in the sentence below.

The old dog the one with the sad brown eyes limped slowly across the field.

(b) What other punctuation marks could you have used to show **parenthesis** in this sentence?

_____ 1 mark

10 Rewrite the sentence below so that it uses **formal language**.

Give us a sec and I'll grab my coat and come with you.

_____

_____ 1 mark

Total marks .... /10   How am I doing? 😊 😐 😣